Block VI   Italian Futurism

Contents

Set reading

Herschel B. Chipp, *Theories of Modern Art,* University of California Press, 1975.

George Heard Hamilton, *Painting and Sculpture in Europe 1880–1940,* Penguin Books, 1981.

You will also need to read the relevant extracts in the *Supplementary Documents.*

Broadcasting

The following programmes are broadcast while you are working on Block VI.

Television programme 14   *Futurism*
Radiovision programme 14   *Der Blaue Reiter*

You should look at the notes and illustrations which accompany these programmes before the broadcasts.

The following broadcasts are also relevant to this block.

Television programme 12   *Cubism 1911–12*
Television programme 13   *Cubism and Dada*
Radiovision programme 25   *Vorticism*

List of illustrations associated with Block VI

(These are provided in separate booklets. You should refer to the captions printed with the plates for full details of the pictures. Those marked with an asterisk are not referred to in the text but relate to the broadcasts.)

Colour plates

1 Boccioni, *The City Rises*
2 Balla, *Streetlight*
3 Carrà, *Funeral of the Anarchist Galli*
4 Boccioni, *The Street Enters the House*
5 Balla, *Girl Running on the Balcony*
6 Boccioni, *States of Mind, the Farewells*
7 Boccioni, *States of Mind, Those Who Go*

8 Boccioni, *States of Mind, Those Who Stay*
9 Boccioni, *States of Mind, the Farewells*
10 Boccioni, *States of Mind, Those Who Go*
11 Boccioni, *States of Mind, Those Who Stay*
*12 Marc, *Fate of the Animals*
*13 Boccioni, *Dynamism of a Soccer Player*

Black-and-white plates

1 Boccioni, *Factories at the Porta Romana*
2 Previati, *La Madonna dei Gigli*
3 da Volpedo, *The Fourth Estate*
4 Balla, *The Workers' Day*
5 Boccioni, *Paolo and Francesca*
6 Boccioni, *Giants and Pygmies*
7 Russolo, *Memories of a Night*
8 Russolo, *Train at Speed*
9 Russolo, *The Revolt*
10 Bragaglia, *The Slap* (photo)

11 Boccioni, *Fusion of Head and Window*
12 Boccioni, *Table plus Bottle plus Houses*
13 Boccioni, *Development of a Bottle in Space*
14 Boccioni, *Synthesis of Human Dynamism*
15 Boccioni, *Muscles at Speed*
16 Boccioni, *Spiral Expansion of Muscles in Movement*
17 Boccioni, *Unique Forms of Continuity in Space*
18 Boccioni, *Elasticity*
19 Carrà, *Speed Decomposes the Horse*
20 Boccioni, *Interior with Two Female Figures*

Introduction

Futurism does not fit easily into a Modernist account of twentieth century art. Filippo Tommaso Marinetti (1876–1944), who founded, sustained and directed the movement, was a writer, rather than a painter, and few of his ideas had any direct connection with painting. The painters whom he attracted to his cause, Umberto Boccioni (1882–1916), Carlo Carrà (1881–1966), Luigi Russolo (1885–1947), Gino Severini (1883–1966) and Giacomo Balla (1871–1958), were recruited after *The Foundation and Manifesto of Futurism* had already been published (20 February, 1909). Their work contains a number of features which have interested Modernist critics, but the themes that bind them together are primarily Marinetti's. These themes include passionate Italian nationalism, militarism, anti-bourgeois rhetoric, an interest in the subject matter of industrialized urban life, cars, aeroplanes and street riots, and a commitment to action rather than autonomous artistic practice. Stated like this, the connection between Futurism and Cubism seems remote, but in fact, for reasons we will have to elucidate, the Futurists appropriated much of the formal repertoire and some of the ideas of Cubism.

Modernist critics have focused on specific 'innovations' of the Futurists which have been built into a particular picture of the development of modern art. We will be looking at some of these in more detail below, but they include the representation of motion, sculptures made of a range of unusual materials, poetry in which grammar and syntax are abandoned, theatrical presentations full of alienating devices, music as 'the art of noise', and so on. These and other 'innovations' have been picked out as relevant for later developments, including Dada, Surrealism, Constructivism, and the New Typography of the 1920s. If we are to make sense of the work of the Futurists, however, we will have to concentrate on the actual conditions in which they operated and identify the causal conditions for specific ideas and artistic practices.

The first difficulty facing the historian of Futurism is in trying to assimilate the flood of written material produced by the Futurists, and in particular Marinetti, and evaluating it as a body of 'explanation' of the paintings. The problem stems partly from the fact that the Futurist manifestoes invariably preceded the work they supposedly 'explain', and often appear to be more comprehensible as independent pieces of creative writing. Art historians usually complain about the lack of written and coherent testimony from the painters being studied — however, in this case the opposite is nearer the mark. Marinetti ran the publicity machine of Futurism like a business, and exacted a similar 'professionalism' from his colleagues. But we will find tensions between the public face of Futurism and the anxieties and concerns of the painters, particularly Boccioni who is the subject of the case study in Part 2. One of the reasons for looking in detail at Futurism is precisely the insight that it gives into how a 'movement' was staged and 'sold' in the early twentieth century. There is none of the 'innocence' here of the artist working away in the studio, leaving it to dealers and critics to explain and defend the work.

Before starting Part 1, which begins by investigating the sources of Marinetti's ideas as expressed in *The Foundation and Manifesto of Futurism,* read the concise introduction to the Futurist section by Joshua C. Taylor (Chipp, pp. 281–3), which introduces the key ideas and personalities of Futurism.

1 Marinetti and the context of Futurism

Now turn to *The Foundation and Manifesto of Futurism* (Chipp, pp. 284–9). Note that the text consists of two main sections, the second beginning with the numbered paragraphs on p. 286. This latter portion had already been published by Marinetti, in January 1909, as a preface to a book of poems by Enrico Cavàcchioli. On 20 February, 1909, the full text was published on the front page of *Le Figaro,* then as now a major circulation newspaper in Paris. It is difficult to imagine a comparable statement receiving such treatment today at the hands of the editor of *The Daily Telegraph* or *The Times.*

▶ Read *The Foundation and Manifesto of Futurism* now. What is Marinetti's message to artists and writers? How would he like them to change the form and content of their work? ◀

▷ The first point to make is that there is little specifically about art and not much on the details of literary practice. Instead, we are presented with a 'story' which, if we take it seriously at all, contains the suggestion that artists and writers should leave the confines of the salon or studio and 'go down' into the world of the modern city — a world of trams, cars, violence and danger. Writers and artists are exhorted to choose their subject matter accordingly: trams, trains, ocean liners and proletarian crowds. One point comes over clearly — anything to do with the art of the past must be avoided and indeed destroyed. ◁

It is an impassioned piece of writing, based on Marinetti's personal experience. The lush apartment described in the opening lines — representing the 'inherited sloth' of the bourgeoisie — was in fact Marinetti's flat in Milan, inherited from his father, and the smoke-filled atmosphere represents vividly the kind of literary life in which Marinetti had made his name in Paris and Italy. The conversion to a new way of life is symbolized by the furious drive through the night, after which Marinetti pictures himself born again, suckled by the filthy water of a factory ditch which he compares to the Sudanese woman who was his wet nurse in his birthplace, Alexandria. A harsh new reality takes over from the decadent eroticism of his upbringing and early career as a Symbolist writer.

The eleven points of the Manifesto proper (Chipp, p. 286), sketch out very clearly the attitudes of the 'man reborn' into the industrialized twentieth century. They are calculated to offend everyone committed to the status quo, and to attract those looking for change at any price. Notice, though, how Marinetti takes the political sting out of words such as 'struggle' or 'revolt' by avoiding the mention of 'government'; instead, he specifies 'violent assault against unknown forces'. The jumble of violent actions seems contradictory: 'militarism, patriotism, the destructive gesture of the anarchist, the beautiful ideas which kill and the scorn of women'. We will have to discover to which constituents of Italian culture these phrases were addressed. I will be arguing that this and the later Futurist Manifestoes were carefully devised to build a following among specific groups of disaffected French and Italian artists, writers, critics and patrons.

By 1908, Marinetti was already well enough known to be the subject of a literary biography. One of the contributors to this book summed up the situation:

> After a series of articles dedicated to his two latest poems, *La Conquete des Étoiles* ('The Conquest of the Stars') and *Destruction,* in the most important Parisian news-papers, *Le Temps, Le Figaro, Gil Blas, Le Gaulois,* Marinetti has become *the* poet in fashion and, if the great salons of the French and Italian aristocracy, from that of the Princess of Monaco to that of the Countess of Noailles, Paul Adam, Madame Stern, Lady Vittoria Cima and Count Scotti, etc., compete for his impassioned conversation, the great publishing houses fall over themselves to publish his manuscripts.
>
> (U. Notari, in T. Panteo, *Il Poeta Marinetti,* 1908, pp.156–7.)

Now, it is not necessary to know who all these people were to recognize the circles of society in which Marinetti moved and the kind of fashionable career that this extract describes. His success was due partly to his sensational, florid, writing style, full of shocking and erotic images, and partly to a prodigious energy that allowed him to keep up a flood of articles, poems, plays and novels backed up by poetry recitals and a hectic social life. Not the least of his assets was money. He inherited a sizeable fortune from his father, which he liked to claim had been amassed in the brothels of Alexandria. During his father's lifetime, Marinetti had studied law at the Sorbonne, in Paris, turning to literature in his spare time progressively through the 1890s. But, with his father's death, he quickly used his inheritance to found a magazine, *Poesia,* in Milan (1905), which he exploited to establish a chain of con-tacts all over Europe. He published the latest work of Symbolists like Verhaeren, Gustave Kahn, Alfred Jarry, Walt Whitman, and welcomed writers from separatist French movements in Provence and Brittany, many of whom became stout suppor-ters of Futurism. To show how he operated, here is an example (addressed to Cam-ille Le Mercier d'Erm) of a letter sent to a long list of writers, critics and editors, enclosing a copy of *The Foundation and Manifesto of Futurism:*

> Dear colleague,
> I would be most grateful if you would send me your views on our Manifesto of Futurism and your total or partial adherence to it. Awaiting your reply, which will be published in *Poesia,* I remain your humble servant,
> F. T. Marinetti
>
> (Cited in P. A. Jannini, *La Fortuna del Futurismo in Francia,* 1979, p.9.)

Although most of the best known names of European Symbolism are missing from the replies, enough figures of repute took the bait to give Marinetti excellent pub-licity and justify the claim that Futurism was attracting widespread attention. A measure of how well Marinetti judged the critical establishment can be gauged from this response to the Manifesto:

> One is rather taken aback to be told that a literary school can be founded just like that, as in a bargain basement. One thought that it took a little longer, and more real achievement, rather than empty posturing. But a Manifesto will do as long as it is a good one. The Futurist Manifesto is excellent; it is by Marinetti.
>
> ('M.D.' 'Le Futurisme', in *Journal des Débats,* 25 February, 1909, cited in Jannini, p.212.)

The rules of the game had been laid down in the 1890s, by the Symbolists, who had used manifestoes to generate discussion and mobilize supporters, as well as critics. Contemporaries made allowances for colourful personalities like Marinetti, while reserving judgment on the ultimate 'seriousness' of the enterprise. One of Marinetti's keen supporters, the separatist Breton poet Camille Le Mercier d'Erm, gave a balanced judgment in his magazine *Les Argonautes* (February, 1909):

> Stirring things up is good enough for you. You are carried away by the fine com-
> motion you provoke around your name and doctrines. . . . You are delighted if
> anyone takes you seriously but care little if your Futurist Manifesto is rated as
> nothing more than one facet of a well-liked Salon personality.
>
> (Jannini, p.29.)

This is a strange world of wealthy patrons and writers who could afford to publish
their own work with that of their friends and play at founding 'revolutionary movements' and 'schools'.

Another convention of the Parisian literary scene, going back at least as far as
the Romanticism of the 1830s and the opening night of Victor Hugo's *Hernani,* was
the provocation of set-piece scuffles and fights in the theatre. Marinetti's friend
Alfred Jarry, for example, deliberately provoked an uproar on the opening night of
his scatological farce *Ubu Roi* in 1895, with a ten-minute address to the audience
before the first curtain. Marinetti's own derivative version, *Le Roi Bombance,* 1905,
aimed at similar effects, using gross caricatures and obscene language to pillory
church, government and socialism with even-handed aggression. After 1909,
Marinetti perfected a particularly effective weapon for attracting publicity while
asserting a claim for anti-bourgeois, and therefore potentially revolutionary status.
This was the Futurist evening, staged in theatres in France and Italy, preceded by
processions through the streets, and including poetry, the reading of manifestoes
(which have to be understood in this context), short sketches and mimes, outland-
ish music (including the *'intonarumori'* 'art of noise' machines of Russolo) and the
exhibition of paintings on stage. Marinetti stated his aims:

> The Futurist evenings signify precisely the *brutal irruption* of life into art. Artists,
> finally *alive,* no longer isolated on the contemptuous peaks of aestheticism, de-
> mand to collaborate like workers and soldiers in the progress of the world.
>
> (Letter to Carlo Albertini, 1915, in G. Lista, *Marinetti et le Futurisme,* 1977, p. 18).

In Part 3 of this block, we will see how ambiguous the political content of
Marinetti's stance was. However, it had a specific operational value, not only in
securing publicity in circles wider than the purely cultural ones, but as a way of
welding together his group of painters and writers into a solid group made vividly
aware of their oppositional stance before the general public. Making sure that the
Futurists all shared the experience of being pelted with rotten fruit and arrested for
street demonstrations did wonders for convincing all of them that they were doing
something more serious than Salon politics. And like a good commissar, Marinetti
knew how to keep his cadres in order:

> We believe, like Bergson, that life overwhelms intelligence, envelopes and chokes
> that tiny little intelligence. Woe to him who stops or hesitates, to query, to
> discuss or daydream! Let us fight any ideal future liable to weaken our struggle
> today or tomorrow!
>
> (F. Marinetti, 'En cette année Futuriste 1915', in Lista, p.16.)

A few points should be clear by now. The power base on which Marinetti launched
Futurism was his own reputation in the introverted circles of Symbolist literature.
But the direction in which he prompted Futurism was away from these narrow
confines to a potentially mass audience, in which anti-bourgeois slogans and a very
public activity could appear to affect everyone. The Futurist Manifesto itself signals
this move from the very specifically literary world to a wider audience, and the
Futurist evenings were intended to carry this out.

An important feature of Marinetti's claim to remove art from the studio and
salon was his stress on the importance of a subject matter derived from modern
industrialized urban life. Here, too, he did not have to look far for sources among
his Symbolist friends. Many writers, like Maxime du Camp and Emile Verhaeren,
had used the imagery of urban life in their work. And an Italian, Mario Morasso,

published a book in 1905 which included a highly formative passage:

> It has been said of the *Victory of Samothrace* . . . that it expresses the very essence of easy and joyous movement. Well, and this comparison is not meant to be disrespectful, the steel monster [a motor car], as it shakes and shudders under the impulse of its impatiently beating engine, constitutes an equally magnificent demonstration of kinetic power and gives clear expression to the insane speeds of which it is capable.
>
> (M. Morasso, *The New Arm (The Machine)*, 1905, in Lista, p. 15.)

Marinetti's more verbose and graphic rephrasing of this idea is often taken as being one of the most striking images of *The Foundation and Manifesto of Futurism*. Whatever the literary sources of Marinetti's ideas, we must look now at some of the material conditions for Futurism in Italy.

Industrialization in northern Italy

Compared to Britain, France or Germany, Italian industrialization happened late and very rapidly. Although the basis was laid in the forty years after the unification of northern Italy (1860), the main take-off took place after 1895. Some key indices of industrial production show how rapid this growth was:

	1895	1900	1905	1910
Output of pig iron (10^3 tonnes)	9	24	143	353
Output of crude steel (10^3 tonnes)	50	116	270	732
Output of electrical energy (gigawatt hours)	0.03	0.14	0.45	1.30

(Source: B.R. Mitchell, *European Historical Statistics*, 2nd rev. edn. 1981.)

Nevertheless, Italy remained a poor country overall, relying on foodstuffs for exports and depending heavily on industrial imports. Productivity per capita remained half that of France and a third of Britain's until the First World War. Extreme inequalities between regions and classes increased in this period and led to frequent bread riots, especially in the 1890s and in the general strike of September 1904. The economic and political crises of the 1890s, which followed each other with bewildering rapidity, were followed by a period of comparative stability under the successive prime ministerships of Giolitti, and the rapid expansion of the northern Italian industrial towns such as Milan and Turin. Almost constant road works and building construction, with the attendant noise, dust and confusion, were a feature of the period.

▶ Look at *Factories at the Porta Romana* (**Pl. VI. 1**) and *The City Rises* (**Col. pl. VI. 1**). Both were painted in Milan. In what ways do you think that these paintings reflect the industrialization of that city? ◀

▷ In both paintings you can see the evidence of building work in progress. In the black-and-white plate you can see scaffolding on one building and the vacant lots waiting to be developed on the outskirts. You may find it more difficult to pick out the workmen with their cart horses in the colour plate. The paintings can be contrasted in terms of the image they give of building work. The first, with its open spaces and tiny men and women returning from work, appears to stress the dreariness and alienation of the urban dweller in the new suburbs. The second focuses on men and animals in a dramatic composition, representing urban change in terms of violent struggle. As we will see, this comparison marks, among other things, the impact of Marinetti on Boccioni. ◁

Automobiles

The development of the car industry in northern Italy was an important component of Italian industrial expansion. A key aspect of this story is rivalry with France. In 1900, France already had 1,200 automobile agents and 7,000 licensed drivers while, in Italy, a mere 300 cars were being manufactured, relying on French or German engines. By 1903, Italian production reached 1,300 and in 1914, 18,000 cars a year, largely as a result of the growth of Fiat in Turin. 1907 became a prestigious year for Italian car manufacturing, when Fiat won the three major speed and endurance trophies for the first time (The Targa Florio, the Emperor's Cup and the Grand Prix of the Automobile Club of France at Dieppe – see Figure 1). For an

Figure 1 Fiat F–2, 130 h.p., 1907, 16.286 litre, 4 cylinders, 1025 kilos, in which Nazzaro won the Grand Prix of the Automobile Club de France in Dieppe at an average speed of 113.612 k.p.h. (Museo dell'Automobile Carlo Biscaretti di Ruffia, Turin.)

Italian who lived part of the time in Paris, like Marinetti, cars were something to brag about, and he owned a succession of Italian cars, including a Fiat like the one in Figure 2. The stark contrast between the chassis of these machines (Figure 3) and their hand-built coachwork helps to illustrate the point made in the Manifesto 'story'. It takes an effort for us to reconstruct the particular allure of these cars, with their monstrous engines, coach springs, wooden wheels and uncertain brakes. The racing cars, as they hurtled along unmade roads through villages and towns, reaped a death toll every year which, in 1903, during the Paris–Madrid road race, reached such proportions that the event was cancelled when the field reached Bordeaux. This event became known as the 'race to the death', and Marinetti may well have had it in mind while writing the Manifesto. Cars were owned by the wealthy and

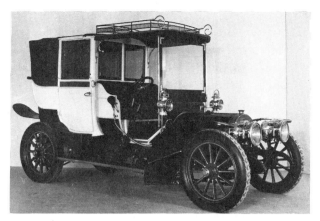

Figure 2 Fiat 18/24 h.p., 1908, 4.5 litre, 4 cylinders, 1000 kilos; (Museo dell'Automobile Carlo Biscaretti di Ruffia, Turin.)

Figure 3 Fiat 35/45 h.p. chassis, 1908, a 6-cylinder version of the model in Figure 2. (Museo dell'Automobile Carlo Biscaretti di Ruffia, Turin.)

powerful, and their victims were usually peasants. Few more poignant images could be found of the destruction of the old agricultural order by the new world of industrialization, and the violence of this aggression forms an essential ingredient in the prose of the Manifesto, even though we are only told of the dogs that died. Ironically, the young Boccioni was a keen illustrator of cars, contributing to their romanticization (Figure 4).

Figure 4 Umberto Boccioni, cover for Avanti della Domenica, *12 November 1905. (Biblioteca Nazionale Centrale, Florence. Photo: Dr. G. B. Pineider.)*

However, if the reality of the growth of the car industry, and its nationalist connotations for Italians, underpins the Manifesto, it hardly characterizes the vocabulary used to describe it. A poem by Marinetti entitled 'Ode to an Automobile', 1908, reveals the allegorical basis of his ideas:

> Headstrong God of a race of steel
> Automobile drunk with space
> Impatiently you paw the ground, the bit between your strident teeth.

An alternative title to this poem was 'To my Pegasus', and if you look back at the Manifesto, you will notice a dual vocabulary used to describe the cars, part allegorical and part realistic. The difficulty of losing the habit of allegory, which also affected car advertising (Figure 5), posters and the design of mascots and trophies (Figure 6), influenced Boccioni as much as Marinetti and must qualify any assessment of Futurism as a realistic response to industrialization.

Figure 5 H. Bellery Dessontaines, advertisement for Automobiles Richard-Brasier, 1904. (Photo: Tim Benton.)

Figure 6 Aucoc, Gordon-Bennett road race trophy. (Photo: Tim Benton.)

Aeroplanes

If a car was a Pegasus, aeroplanes, too, had a Symbolist pedigree. Gabriele D'Annunzio, who was a major figure in Italian literary life, as much for his extravagant lifestyle as for his exotic and decadent poetry and prose, made flying a cult among his admirers. To take one example, Mussolini, then a radical socialist journalist, declared himself a 'D'Annunzian' and in emulation taught himself to fly. For him, aeroplanes represented the triumph of will over the elements, a symbol of progress and the conquest of fear.

> Our age is perhaps even more heroic than Antiquity. Mercantilism has not suffocated the spasm of agonising but healthy adventure. This is a movement towards the acceleration of life. The four primordial elements are now in man's power . . . The dream of Icarus, the dream of all generations, is being translated into reality. Man has conquered the air . . . O Zarathustra, is it perhaps from the precipitous bank of the Sangatte that the dawn of the superman has been announced? Is our painful prehistory finally over?
>
> (B. Mussolini, in *Il Popolo di Trento,* 1909.)

Nietzsche's *Thus Spake Zarathustra,* first published in 1883, had become a key text for many intellectuals irritated by scientific positivism and impatient with parliamentary government and bourgeois values. In Alfred Jarry's *Surmâle* (1902), a Nietzschian work that much impressed his friend Marinetti, the relation between man and machine is seen in similar terms:

> In this age when metal and mechanics are all-poweful, man, in order to survive, must become stronger than the machine, just as he has had to become stronger than the beasts.

The ghastly consequences of pitting men against machines in the First World War gave this kind of talk a new meaning. In fact, it was the Italian army that first used aeroplanes to attack infantry. During the Libyan campaign of 1911, half a dozen Bleriots and other fragile contraptions were used to drop grenades and hand bombs on the Turkish trenches, with a psychological impact out of all proportion to the casualties caused. Marinetti was there as a journalist, and seized on the event as confirmation of his theories. Here was 'man made powerful by the machine', which he had celebrated in characteristic vein in 1909:

> Here it is, my own multi-cellular biplane, steered by the tail: 100 HP, 8 cylinders, 80 kilogrammes . . . Between my feet I have a tiny machine gun which I can fire with a steel button.
>
> (F. Marinetti, 'Let's Murder the Moonbeams', 1909.)

With this phallic weapon, Marinetti swoops into the heart of battle, into

> . . . the furious coitus of war, gigantic vulva stirred by the friction of courage.
>
> (*Ibid.*)

It wasn't until Marinetti's conversion to Fascism in the 1920s, and the so-called 'second Futurism', that all this imagery came to be embodied literally in a school of painting (*Aeropittura*) (Figure 7) and poetry (*Aeropoesia*), based on the imagery of the Fascist superman surveying a world of pygmies through his bomb-sight.

I have introduced you to some of Marinetti's views and the context of Futurist imagery, because we now have to consider its impact on the Futurist painters, and Boccioni in particular. We will return to the content of Futurist ideology in Part 3, and consider to what extent the Futurist painters shared these views.

Figure 7 (a) Ambrosi, Il Duce (Aeropittura), *1939. Superimposed on Mussolini's face are a number of Fascist architectural projects. (b) Dino delle Site,* Flight of a Nocturnal Patrol, *1939. (Photos: Tim Benton.)*

The Futurist painters

Read Hamilton's section on Futurism (pp. 279–91), concentrating on his attempt to 'place' Futurism in the history of modern art. Don't worry about his detailed description of Futurist ideas and paintings, as we will be returning to these below. Hamilton summarizes his treatment of Futurism by stating (p.291):

> But they deserve their moment in history for their concern with motion and their attempt to represent it through unconventional materials and techniques. Their recognition of the inherent restlessness of modern life expressed in man's obsession with technology added a new psychological dimension to modern art.

In these two sentences is an apparent contradiction between a concern with purely painterly practices and an ideological interest that we have seen to be central to Marinetti's own interests.

▶ How does Hamilton support these assertions and what qualifications does he make about the status of Futurism? ◀

▷ The 'concern with motion' is illustrated partly through the Marinettian stress on motor cars and *'velocità'* and partly through the painters' attempts to translate this into form, e.g. Russolo's *The Revolt* or Boccioni's *Unique Forms of Continuity in Space* (Hamilton, Figures 168 and 171). We will look in some detail at the latter work, and Boccioni's attempts to explain the ideas behind it. However, it may have occurred to you that there is no obvious connection between these rather odd painterly interests and the very immediate concerns of Marinetti — driving fast cars and flying aeroplanes. Hamilton (p.287) refers to the 'unconventional materials' of Boccioni's sculptures, relating them to a 'proto-Dada accumulation of scrap' on the one hand and Cubist *papier collés* on the other. Elsewhere Hamilton notes the dependence of the Futurists on Cubist techniques and suggests that the Futurist painters had difficulty finding 'a new synthesis of form and feeling' (p.290). Instead, he characterizes 'Futurist painting, even Boccioni's best', as 'an unstable combination of Neo-Impressionist brushwork, harsh Expressionist colour, and Cubist drawing'. The criticism is stated in art-historical terms — a question of originality and influences — rather than as a judgment on the effectiveness of the paintings in expressing Futurist ideology. ◁

One of the problems, here, is that Boccioni himself seems to have accepted rather similar assumptions. In his writings he makes it clear that he intended to take on and defeat the Cubists on their own ground in Paris. I want to argue that this competitive attitude, rooted in Marinetti's aggressive nationalism and provocative rhetoric, necessarily diverted the Futurist painters from pursuing the line Marinetti laid out for them, which concentrated on celebrating the new world of industrial change. It is important to understand the dilemma of the Futurists who, unlike Marinetti, had not already made a reputation, but who saw themselves as provincial artists struggling to get to grips with the new developments in Paris.

Italian Divisionism and Futurism

Fundamental to any discussion of Italian art of the early twentieth century is an understanding of the uneasy proximity of three interests: the search for a 'scientific' basis for painting, a Symbolist approach to subject matter and a political ideology broadly of the left, ranging from the humanitarian socialism of Tolstoy or William Morris to the violent anarchism of Georges Sorel or Bakunin. All three ingredients, not obviously compatible, already formed part of the circle of Vittore Grubicy de Dragon in the 1890s, whose gallery supported the two best-known Italian Divisionists, Giovanni Segantini and Gaetano Previati.

Boccioni was particularly impressed by Previati and his technical treatise, *Principi Scientifici del Divisionismo* (2 vols., 1905–6), visiting the old man on two occasions and recording in his diary his struggle to master the scientific principles involved. The Divisionist theory which Previati summarized in his book was essentially positivist — based on the writings of Chevreul, Rood and Henry. In essence the theory sought to discover, by experiment, fixed laws relating colours, lines and shapes and their various juxtapositions to specific feelings or emotional states. Charles Henry's 'aesthetic protractor' (1888) and 'chromatic circle' (1889) purported to specify precisely the emotional equivalent of lines at different angles and different colours which could be read off and combined across a polarity ranging from the 'dynamogenic' to the 'inhibitory'. If taken literally, this kind of theory implied that all ideas can be stimulated by physical correlatives and that these need not have any support in representational subject matter. But the Divisionists, and the Futurists after them, accepted neither that subject matter was irrelevant nor that the positivist view of the world was adequate. On the contrary, Segantini and Previati continually tackled themes that Grubicy described as 'abstract, mystical, indefinite in their parts'. Previati's *Maternity* (1891) is characteristic of the kind of subject that should be treated:

> . . . in a kind of complex, fluctuating, synthetic combination of forms and colours which barely allow a glimpse of the symbolism or the ideas, either musical or supernatural, in my mind.
>
> (V. Grubicy, *Cronaca d'Arte*, 1891, p.181.)

Previati's *La Madonna dei Gigli* (1894) (**Pl.VI.2**) is characteristic of his style. This is far removed from the language of Seurat or Cézanne, and the Italian critics also perceived the work of the French Impressionists and Post-Impressionists differently to most French critics. Ardengo Soffici, for example, who was to become a supporter of Futurism, wrote up Cézanne in Symbolist terms:

> He could bathe the animate and inanimate beings in his compositions in an atmosphere of spiritual unity. Men, animals, trees and skies were no longer represented as isolated or fragmentary elements but reunited in a harmony of lines and forms dominated by his will and constrained to reveal a vision which was his and from which they came to be reassembled in the world of appearances.
>
> (A. Soffici, *La Voce*, pp.202–7.)

And he contrasted Cézanne with the Impressionists:

> It transpires, in fact, that all that work [the Impressionists'] is above all empirical and descriptive, and that what it lacks is the mark of that divine will which draws to itself the forms of things, analyses them, concentrates them and sends them out again, transformed to lie forever in the universe – what is known as *style*.
>
> (*Ibid.*)

Soffici's writing reflects the idealist attitudes in Italian thought, the most influential exponent being the philosopher Benedetto Croce, who reinterpreted the Hegelian tradition in Italian terms. In an article on Impressionism, Soffici echoed the language of Jules Romains' 'Unanimism' which you have met in Block V. Marinetti and Severini both frequented the Closerie des Lilas group in Paris and Marinetti made Romains' *La Vie Unanime* (1908) known in Italy. According to Soffici, the Impressionists' discovery was that:

> One world does not stop where another starts. . . the one extends into the other like drops of water in a river, that the universe is altogether harmonious, that life circulates everywhere. . . They realized that, for example, a man, a horse, a field, a wall are *alive* equally for the artist and that therefore the wall and field should not serve only as a backdrop to the man and horse but should harmonize poetically with them in an expressive whole.
>
> (A. Soffici, *La Voce*, March 1909.)

This approach was discussed in a different context in Block V. We will find very similar language in Boccioni's *Technical Manifesto of Futurist Painting*.

The third ingredient of Italian Divisionism, a political commitment to humanitarian socialism and anarchism, was particularly evident in the group of painters associated with Giuseppe Pellizza da Volpedo. Some of these artists were directly involved politically.

Emilio Longoni was prosecuted for incitement to class hatred for his *Reflections of a Starving Man* (1893), and Plinio Nomellini was imprisoned after a famous trial in which he was convicted of participating in an anarchist group led by Luigi Galleani. Most of the Italian Divisionists, like their contemporaries in France, were sympathetic to these causes — Giuseppe Pellizza da Volpedo appearing as witness on Nomellini's behalf. Pellizza's *The Fourth Estate*, 1901 (**Pl.VI.3**) began as a commemoration of a massacre of workers in Milan in 1898. Secure with a private income, and living in the agricultural town of Volpedo away from the harshest repression of workers' strikes in the last years of the century, Pellizza committed himself to humanitarian socialism, joining the Peasants' and Workers' Mutual Aid Society in 1890. Of an earlier version of this picture, Pellizza wrote that it was:

An attempt. . . to raise myself above the vulgarity of subjects which do not conform to a strong idea. I am attempting Social painting. . . . A crowd of people, workers of the soil, who are intelligent, strong, robust, united, advance like a torrent overthrowing every obstacle in its path, thirsty for justice.

(Quoted in *Post-Impressionism* catalogue, p.246.)

Pellizza's experience and commitment were rooted in the effects of industrialization and changing economic conditions in the countryside. But the social commitment shared by the group also influenced artists determined to focus on urban subject matter, of whom Balla was a significant example. His painting now known as *The Workers' Day* (**Pl. VI.4**) combines this urban subject matter with an experimental approach to Divisionist technique. The large canvas on the right seems to have been exhibited first, on its own, in 1904, to be joined by the two other parts in 1907, when it was entitled *They Work, Eat and Go Home*.

Contemporary viewers were aware that most building workers servicing the industrial expansion of the developed cities came from the poorer agricultural regions of southern Italy. Balla taught Boccioni and Severini, whom he befriended in 1900, that urban life was a worthy and necessary subject for a socially committed artist and that the techniques of Divisionism could provide a powerful medium for representing the new conditions of urban life. His *Lampada—Studio di luce* (*Streetlight*), of 1909 (**Col. pl. VI.2**) is characteristic of his attempt to reconcile technical and social interests. Later, he wrote of it:

This painting, as well as being original as a work of art, is also scientific, because I tried to represent light by separating the colours of which it is composed. It is of great historical interest both for its technique and for its subject. No-one at that date (1909) thought that a banal electric light could be a motif for pictorial inspiration. On the contrary, for me, there was a subject in it, and it was the attempt to represent light, and above all, to show that the romantic moonlight had been superseded by the light of the modern electric bulb. That is, the end of romanticism in art. From my painting came the phrase, 'let's kill the moonbeams'.

(Cited in M. F. dell'Arco, *Balla Pre-Futurista,* 1970.)

Balla's explanation shows how important subject matter was for the Italian Divisionists. The lamp standard shown was one of the first installed in Rome (in the Piazza Termini in 1904), and the subject reflected a key ingredient in Italian industrial expansion: hydroelectric power — a crucial alternative to expensive imported coal and the object of important governmental investment. It is no accident that the Futurist architect Sant'Elia devoted many of his architectural sketches to studies of hydroelectric power stations.

By 1909, then, the Italian Divisionists, including the painters who were to become Futurists, were already working through a range of subjects reflecting urban change and industrialization. They were thus susceptible to the impact of Marinetti's ideas, although their political views were very different from his.

2 Umberto Boccioni

Figure 8 Boccioni in his studio in Milan (c. 1914) with a plaster version of the artist's mother. (Photo: courtesy of Zeno Birolli.)

Boccioni has been selected for detailed attention partly because he was the accepted leader of the painters and partly because his theoretical views were more developed than those of his colleagues. In 1908, Boccioni was still looking for a settled style of work. Paintings like *Factories at the Porta Romana* (**Pl. VI. 1**), which we have already looked at, come directly from the teaching of Balla and the 'political' Divisionists. We will find, in Part 3, that Boccioni considered himself 'a Marxist' and shared the political objectives of Balla's friends. At the same time, he was experimenting with different kinds of Symbolism. A pen drawing, *Beata Solitudo,* combines the imagery of Pre-Rapahelitism, Beardsley, French and Belgian Symbolism and topical images such as the Wright brothers' flyer and a dirigible. In the same year (1908), a painting variously entitled *Il Sogno* (*The Dream*) or *Paolo and Francesca* (**Pl. VI. 5**) shows him in full flow as a romantic Symbolist. In his diary, Boccioni summed up his predicament, caught between Previati's scientific principles and his own idealistic tendencies:

> All modern art seems old to me. I want something new, expressive, fantastic. . . It seems to me today that, while scientific analysis shows us the Universe in a marvellous way, art should make itself the interpreter of a fateful and powerful resurgence of a new *idealist positivism.* It seems to me that art and artists are today in conflict with science.
>
> (Boccioni, *Diary,* 14 March 1907, cited in Z. Birolli (ed.) *Boccioni: Scritti editi e inediti,* Feltrinelli, Milan, 1971, p.236.)

Boccioni's letters and diary confirm that Marinetti's Manifesto seemed to him to offer a seductive mixture of violent idealism clothed in the rhetoric of material progress. Whatever scruples he may have had about Marinetti's iconoclasm (Boccioni's diaries and letters are full of references to Michelangelo and the Italian

18

masters) and militaristic nationalism, he responded enthusiastically to the challenge
to assert a modern school of Italian painting. Marinetti offered a route out of the
Italian backwater. The first chance to formulate the principles of this new school of
painting came with the *Technical Manifesto of Futurist Painting,* 11 April 1910
(Chipp, pp.289–93).

▶ Read this document now. Bearing in mind what you know of the Italian critical
tradition and Boccioni's sense of being 'in conflict with science', how does this text
illuminate the problems of perception, reality and painterly technique? ◀

▷ The 'growing need of truth' is stated at the outset as a motivating force behind
Futurist art, and there are references to 'results analogous to those of the X-rays',
the 'vivifying current of science', 'the persistency of an image upon the retina', and
'the material needs of our time'. All this sounds positivist. On the other hand, the
rest of the Technical Manifesto is written in terms hardly compatible with science:
'The dynamic sensation itself (made eternal)', 'Space no longer exists', the 'persis-
tent symbols of universal vibration', 'the motor bus rushes into the houses which it
passes', and so on. You will probably have noticed the similarities with Soffici's
descriptions of Cézanne and the Impressionists: 'To paint a human figure you must
not paint it; you must render the whole of its surrounding atmosphere'. Behind the
language, deliberately intended (at Marinetti's insistence) to shock and amaze an
audience at a public reading of the Manifesto, we can detect the typically Italian
translation of Impressionist techniques into expressive conventions intended to en-
able the soul to be 'purified'. The claim that 'we shall henceforward put the spectator in the centre of the picture' reveals the distance between Boccioni and the
Impressionists whose techniques he advocated. ◁

Between April 1910 and the summer of 1911, the Futurist painters tried to put
into effect the heady but woolly programme that they had devised. A serious problem in Italy was the lack of exhibiting opportunities outside the conventional Salons
and the Venice Biennale. Severini and Boccioni had already organized a small *'mostra dei rifiutati'* (similar to the *Salon des Refusés*) in the foyer of the *Teatro Nazionale* in
Rome, in 1905, after their paintings had been rejected by the jury of the *Società
degli Amatori e Cultori di Belle Arti.* And Carrà had had the experience of reforming a
traditional art lovers' exhibiting society, the *Famiglia Artistica,* in Milan so that it
accepted a wider range of painters, with the support of left-wing groups. An important event in Milan which developed these principles further was the *Mostra d'Arte
Libera* (Free Art Exhibition), in April 1911. Hamilton refers to this on page 282,
drawing a parallel with Kandinsky and Marc's interest in 'primitive art'.

The exhibition was an enormous affair, with 800 paintings, of which the Futurists contributed 50. It was organized by a philanthropic organization, the *Società
Umanitaria,* of the *Casa del Lavoro* in Milan. Profits from the show went to the *Casa
del Lavoro* for the benefit of the unemployed, and the support of anarchists and
syndicalists reflected the radical basis of the idea. There was no jury (very unusual at
the time in Italy) and the invitation stressed not only the belief that ordinary
working people (and the unemployed) would appreciate the work, but that they
would be willing to contribute as well.

> Part of our aim is not to mount one of the usual exhibitions of art but, instead, to
> show that the artistic sense, normally held to be the privilege of a few, is innate in
> human nature and that the forms which are thus manifested simply reflect a grea-
> ter or lesser sensibility in the creator.

Children and workers were called on to exhibit and it was hoped that 'a more
ingenuous, instinctive, sincere art would evolve, taken back to its healthy roots'.

Marinetti was quick to declare that workers and children understood Futurism better than the bourgeois and the intellectuals, but the real basis for Futurist involvement in this exhibition was the anarchist and socialist interests of Carrà and Boccioni.

Boccioni's *The City Rises* (originally entitled *Lavoro (Work)*) (**Col.pl.VI.**1) and Carrà's *Funeral of the Anarchist Galli* (**Col.pl.VI.**3) were both exhibited at the exhibition (see Hamilton, pp.281–2). On the face of it, both paintings fit well with Marinetti's insistence on portraying 'the great masses agitated by work, pleasure or revolt. . . the multicoloured and polyphonic surf of revolutions in modern capitals'. And Carrà later described how he witnessed Galli's funeral:

> And it was the memory of that dramatic scene which led me to use in the *Technical Manifesto of Futurism* the phrase 'We will place the spectator in the centre of the painting'.

Most critics accept, in fact, that the main author of the Technical Manifesto was Boccioni rather than Carrà, but the recollection helps us to contextualize its language: vivid experiences, particularly with a politically charged connotation, were very important to the Futurists in the early stages. Boccioni described his painting, in the catalogue of the Sackville Gallery Exhibition of Futurism in London (March 1912), in more Symbolist terms:

> The immense horses symbolize the growth and the desperate labour of the great city, thrusting her scaffoldings (*sic*) towards the sky.

Preliminary sketches for the painting, some of them organized in triptych format (**Pl.VI.**6) and labelled *'Dawn'*, *'Day'*, *'Night'*, show that an important element of the idea was the struggle between the huge cart horse and a group of workers – an observation of anecdotal origin. This detail is progressively eliminated in the sketches, and the form of the horse takes on a strange shape, like a winged Pegasus, the 'wing' growing out of the bulky yoke used to harness the horses. Boccioni appears to want to create an impression of an indefinable force of tremendous power. He described it, rather elliptically, as:

> A canvas 3 metres by 2 where I have sought a great synthesis of labour, light and movement. Perhaps it is a transitional work, and *I believe it to be one of the last!* (original emphasis). It was made completely without a model, and all the skills of the craft are sacrificed in the ultimate cause of emotion.
>
> (Letter to Barbantini, September, 1910, in G. Ballo, *Boccioni,* p.220.)

He cannot have meant that he did not make studies for the painting, since several realistic sketches by him of horses of this kind exist. There is even a photograph of Boccioni drawing one of these cart horses. His point seems to be that realistic detail is not important, compared to the emotion. The phrase 'synthesis of labour, light and movement', combining form and content, reminds us precisely of the combination of Symbolism and scientific Divisionism in the work of Previati.

For a rather different idea of how the Technical Manifesto might have been carried out, look at Russolo's *Memories of a Night* (**Pl.VI.**7) exhibited at the Free Art Exhibition in Milan.

▶ What correspondences can you find between this painting and the Technical Manifesto? ◀

▷ In some ways, there appear to be more direct parallels here. The multiple legs of a horse seem to echo the 'twenty legs' of the Manifesto, and there is even a juxtaposition with the head of a woman, referring to the 'horse which passes at the end of the street' seen on 'the cheek of the person with whom we were talking'. Russolo also appears to have attempted to depict 'the street pavement, soaked by rain beneath the glare of electric lamps . . . gapes to the very center of the earth'. The 'heart-rending expressions of colour' could be referred to the electric lamps in the picture. The superimposition of different fragments of image, silhouetted figures, a face, a profile, a crowd of people, fits the general tenor of 'dynamism' and the changing states of images, but it also refers to the Bergsonian notion of memory which will be given verbal expression in the 'Exhibitors to the Public', 1912 (Chipp, p.296, first para.). ◁

Of the Futurists, Russolo was the one who responded most programmatically to the precise terms of the Technical Manifesto, often devising motifs that the others would take up in their own work. For example, his *Train at Speed* (Pl. VI.8) was significant in introducing to the group the device that soon became a cliché for representing not only actual motion but the 'sensation of dynamism'. He made a compositional device of the cartoonist's and illustrator's favourite trick, 'speed lines', which, like an atmospheric bow-wave, suggest rushing wind and speed through the air. In his *The Revolt* (Pl. VI.9, and Hamilton, Figure 168), these 'speed lines' are given a more conceptual and symbolic meaning, spelled out in the Sackville Gallery catalogue (London, March, 1912):

> The collision of two forces, that of the revolutionary element made up of enthusiasm and red lyricism against the force of inertia and reactionary resistance of tradition. The angles are the vibratory waves of the former force in motion. The perspective of the houses is destroyed just as a boxer is bent double by receiving a blow in the wind (*sic*).

The rather diagrammatic form of the painting hardly carries the levels of meaning that the catalogue entry reads into it. But the Futurist painters eagerly tried to develop the sophistication of their work to match the intentions of Marinetti's and Boccioni's respective Manifestoes. They saw the need to come to terms with the more complex and ambiguous formal repertoire of Cubism, and we must now see how the Futurists tried to achieve this. That they felt compelled to do so reflects the power of Paris as a recognized centre of modern art. A key factor that brought this home to the Italian painters was the well-informed journalism of Soffici in *La Voce*. It could be argued that the need to engage with Cubism was felt to be an *artistic* imperative by the Futurists, but that this made it harder for them to carry out the programme laid out in their manifestoes

In the summer of 1911, Severini paid a visit to Milan and was scathing about the work of his friends, comparing it unfavourably to the latest developments of Cubism and Parisian criticism. Severini's views were backed up by an influential article by Soffici in *La Voce,* in August 1911, dealing with Picasso and Braque. Soffici referred to an article in a French magazine on the Cubists (R. Allard in *Les Marchés du Sud-Ouest,* June, 1911), in which was illustrated one of Delaunay's *Eiffel Tower* paintings (Hamilton, Figure 154) and Léger's *Nudes in the Forest* (see Col. pl. V.8) among others. Apparently on the basis of these illustrations, but without having seen any Cubist paintings at first hand, Boccioni made some tentative experiments with the Cubist method during the autumn of 1911, before his trip to Paris. His *The Street Enters the House* (Col. pl. VI.4) was begun and perhaps finished before going.

▶ What ideas can you find in this painting that reflect the Futurist Manifestoes, and what formal influences from Cubism? ◀

▷ The subject matter still comes out of the set of ideas that had prompted *The City Rises* — represented by building work, noise, confusion in the city. But these ideas, although still present in *The Street Enters the House,* are less prominent: instead of the apocalyptic horse, we are shown the back view of a woman. And we can find several direct echoes of Boccioni's Technical Manifesto: 'To paint a human figure you must not paint it; you must render the whole of its surrounding atmosphere', and 'the motor bus rushes into the houses which it passes, and in their turn the houses throw themselves upon the motor bus and are blended with it'. The idea that all sensations somehow flow together and produce a whole which no fixed perspective or static image can convey seems to be expressed in the painting by the confusion of imagery and rather literal interpenetration of forms. Notice, for example, the horse, bottom right, whose struggling form has been displaced from the street below to join the figure on the balcony. From Delaunay, Léger and the Abbaye de Créteil painters Boccioni seems to have grasped the idea that things should be shown simultaneously from different viewpoints – there appear to be three versions of the woman on the balcony, one from each side. The houses on the right echo very graphically the Delaunay *Eiffel Tower* that Boccioni had seen in reproduction. But Boccioni's painting combines rather realistic details — men, horses, scaffolding poles, houses — with this new-found language of Cubism, with inconsistent results. ◁

Of course, it may well be a distortion to judge *The Street Enters the House* solely in terms of incompetent Cubism. When this painting was exhibited in Paris, in February 1912, the catalogue included an explanation of the content and meaning (Chipp, p.295, bottom paragraph).

▶ Read 'The Exhibitors to the Public' (Chipp, pp.294–8), concentrating particularly on the parts relating to this picture. What criticism of Cubism is Boccioni making, and how does this painting exemplify an alternative approach? ◀

▷ The attack on Cubism is aimed at the 'static', 'frozen', 'traditional' aspects of Cubist technique and their devaluation of 'the subject' which Boccioni sees as 'a sort of masked academism (*sic*)'. The neutral subject matter of the Cubists — the figure, still life — and their concern with analytical form is contrasted with the Futurists' own 'absolutely modern sensation', the 'style of motion', 'the simultaneousness of states of mind', the 'dynamic sensation', or 'interior force' of objects. Note that although Boccioni refers to the theories of Henry — 'all inanimate objects display by their lines calmness or frenzy, sadness or gaiety' — he quickly dispels any scientific claims for these correlations between form and emotion by stating that the 'decomposition' of a form following the 'tendencies of its forces' is 'not governed by fixed laws but varies according to the characteristic personality of the object and the emotions of the onlooker'. Like his phrase 'idealist positivism' which we have already come across, Boccioni's 'physical transcendentalism' attempts to link incompatible notions, the physical and the metaphysical, the idealist and the positivist. *The Street Enters the House* reflects a similarly incompatible mixture of intentions in seeking to portray real physical changes to the city while dissolving the reality of the image in a welter of 'visual sensations . . . freed from accepted logic'. ◁

At one point Boccioni reveals how he thought of the Futurists' position compared with that of the Impressionists (Chipp, p. 296, eighth para.). Impressionist 'reflections of light' are contrasted with 'a real competition of lines and by real conflicts of planes, following the emotional law which governs the picture'. Further down, a passage that fits Carrà's *Funeral of the Anarchist Galli* refers to 'the general law of violence of the picture'. Futurism is Impressionism plus violence, conflict, emotion. To understand the intellectual context that made this seem respectable, we have to turn again to Bergson, whose ideas and influence were outlined in Block V. His *Introduction à la Metaphysique* was translated into Italian (1907) by Papini (who was converted to Futurism alongside his Florentine colleague, Soffici). But Boccioni owned Bergson's more influential work, *Matière et Mémoire* (*Matter and Memory*) (1896) in the original French and made notes on it. Bertrand Russell's succinct summary of Bergson's ideas introduces the key issue:

> Bergson's philosophy, unlike most of the systems of the past, is dualistic: the world, for him, is divided into two disparate portions, on the one hand life, on the other matter, or rather that inert something which the intellect views as matter. The whole Universe is the clash and conflict of two opposite motions: life, which climbs upward, and matter, which falls downward.
>
> (B. Russell, *History of Western Philosophy*, pp.756–65.)

Corresponding to this dualism is a distinction between *intellect*, which concerns itself with matter and space, and *intuition*, which alone can grasp life in its continuous flux in time. Bergson coined the phrase '*l'élan vital*' (the vital impulsion) to describe this great flood of the life-force which, in conflict with matter, marks the evolution of man as a higher being. Many of Bergson's ideas deal directly with the problem of perception and how we know the world. If we want to get beyond mere superficiality (the kind of knowledge needed by the body for routine survival), Bergson thinks that we have to make a great effort of imaginative intuition, 'the sympathy by means of which one places oneself inside an object in order to coincide with what is unique about it'. You might think that this sounds more like mysticism than philosophy, but it helps us to understand Boccioni's reference to the need to place the soul of the spectator in the centre of the picture. In this context, Boccioni's statement turns out to correspond to a theory of knowledge (Bergson's) rather than the kind of experience recounted by Carrà

Bergson was also exercised by the problem of space and time. Space, according to him, belongs on the side of the measurable, finite, material side of the world. Time, on the other hand, belongs to the vital, fluid, intangible and intuitive side. He concludes that you cannot stop time, so there can be no past, present or future. We live in the past in the memory, as a continuous flow of experience. Bergson gives the example of an arm movement, from point A to point B. We experience the movement as continuous, and think of the time taken by the movement as 'duration', unbroken, not jerking like the frames of a cine camera from one 'present' to the next. From this plausible observation, Bergson builds 'duration' into 'the very stuff of reality, which is perpetual becoming, never something made' (as Bertrand Russell put it). The dualism intellect/intuition and space/time is extended by Bergson into memory. In *Matière et Mémoire,* he distinguished between two ways of knowing the world. Perception, he argues, deals with that purely physical contact with matter which the body depends on for survival and which is the stuff of habit: avoiding obstacles, finding things. For more important matters, however, Bergson argued that all knowledge passes through a special faculty, which is memory. This is an imaginative grasp of the duration of time that can somehow be outside the present and uncontaminated by matter and the purely material facts of perception. The mind, through intuition and memory, sees through superficial reality to the essence of things. Notice (Chipp, p.296, 1st line) how Boccioni has tried to grapple with these ideas. To see how he worked them up into a general theory of 'dynamism' and motion, read the extracts from his book, *Futurist Painting and Sculpture,* 1914 (*Supplementary Documents*).

▶ Read these extracts now. What echoes of Bergson's ideas can you find here? ◀

▷ Boccioni's distinction between 'quantitative study' and 'qualitative study' corresponds to Bergson's dualist distinctions between intellect and intuition. Boccioni refers to 'absolute motion' as the 'breathing or heart-beat of the object', which again is a way of describing Bergson's notion of the *'élan vital'*. The whole stress on motion and dynamism derives from Bergson's peculiar conception of reality as a struggle between life and matter. The stress on the fourth dimension relates to the importance of time and duration in Bergson's philosophy, being essential to his understanding of how the mind intuits reality. The passage contrasting the 'cinematographic idea' or 'the tracing of an object from point A to point B' picks up Bergson's terms precisely. ◁

In fact, the issue of 'cinematography' as opposed to 'absolute' motion was one which surfaced in debate amongst the Futurists themselves. Balla made a number of experiments to portray motion as a series of superimposed states, no doubt drawing encouragement from the Technical Manifesto: 'Thus a running horse has not four legs but twenty, and their movements are triangular', which sounds like a purely cinematographic representation of movement. His *Girl Running on the Balcony,* 1912 **(Col. pl.VI.5)** is exactly like this, indicating the successive positions of the body as if several instantaneous images had been superimposed. But although Balla's technique, using an overall pattern of brick-like strokes, disguises the literalness of the idea, Boccioni criticized Balla for his 'cinematographic' approach and his inability to grasp, as Bergson would have insisted, the flow of motion as an unbroken stream of action. Similar charges were levelled against Anton Bragaglia, a photographer in Rome who was encouraged by Marinetti to exhibit and publish his 'photo-dynamic' works **(Pl.VI.10)**. These were images made by allowing a figure to move from one fixed position to another, the movement being registered as a blur on the photographic plate. This time, it was not the jerking of the image from one 'present' to the next, but the whole question of *'movimentismo'* which Boccioni objected to . He wanted Futurist dynamism to be understood in terms of Bergson's 'memory' and 'duration', a question of intuiting the inner vitality of things, rather than attempting to portray moving objects. It should be clear by now why Boccioni was stung by Roger Allard's jibe that the Futurists 'had a cinematographer in the belly' (*Revue Independante,* August 1911).

Futurism and Cubism

The theory of dynamism and motion which Boccioni gradually developed between 1911 and 1914 was aimed primarily at pointing up what he perceived to be the weakness of the Cubists — their analytical, intellectual dependence on *perception* and *matter* — to which he contrasted the Futurists' 'higher', 'intuitive grasp of the world (but recall Block V, Part 3, for contemporary views on this). When, in October 1911, Boccioni, Carrà and, probably, Russolo, visited Paris with Marinetti to see for themselves what the Cubists were up to, they all rather radically changed their technique. The trip was to reconnoitre the ground for the exhibition that was eventually held in February 1912 at the Bernheim–Jeune Gallery. They met Picasso and Braque (who was a neighbour of Severini's) and Apollinaire, Metzinger, Gleizes, Le Fauconnier and Léger. They were greeted with amused condescension and scepticism (see Appendix C), leaving Boccioni and Carrá determined to master the difficult theories and practices of Cubism and show the supremacy of Futurist ideas. A clear indicator of the effects of the trip can be had from comparing the early and final stages of the triptych *States of Mind* by Boccioni (**Col.pls. VI.6 –11**). As early as 29 May 1911, when Boccioni gave his lecture to the *Circolo Artistico* in Rome, the painting was far enough advanced to be described: the intention was to paint 'pure sensation', he maintained, rather than conventional perception. In 'The Exhibitors to the Public' (Chipp, p.297), there is a description of the painting that stresses the formal devices used to arouse specific emotions.

▶ Compare the oil sketches for *The States of Mind,* completed before the trip to Paris, with the final version exhibited in Paris in February 1912. What effect does the addition of Boccioni's notions of Cubist techniques have on the work? ◀

▷ The clearest example is perhaps *The Farewells.* In the sketch, the flame-like streaks of colour diagonally slanting across the canvas dominate any sense of the materiality of objects. In the finished work, Cubist-like fragmentation gives precise clues to the representational content of the scene. The stencilled number, the clear suggestion of the smokestack, buffer, the rounded form of the boiler and cab of the engine, the sections of steelwork and the trail of sparks all give us an idea of the direction of the train and its location. The figures, painted in a subdued green colour, can be recognized as embracing couples. ◁

The machine, as symbol of industrialization, 'progress' and emigration, carries meanings beyond the anecdotal event of departure. A similar comparison could be made in the case of *Those Who Go,* where the sketch wipes out the figures themselves, representing their confused view of houses and telegraph poles rushing past the window. In the finished version, the heads of the passengers can be perceived, some of them apparently shown in more than one position. The stencilled 'I' and 'III' indicate First and Third Class carriages. And in *Those Who Stay,* the finished picture, while still retaining the depressing vertical striation, gives us glimpses of the figures treated almost as if they were being unravelled into strips.

It is clear, then, that the contact with Cubism encouraged Boccioni to introduce a new set of technical and formal devices into his work. With these devices, based on the juxtaposition of sharply defined fragments of perception, came a contradiction with the stress on 'dynamic continuity' dependent on his understanding of Bergson's theories of memory, duration and the *'élan vital'*. If Boccioni criticized the Cubists for their 'translation onto the picture plane of the planes of the object. . .' it is difficult to see how he could assimilate the same techniques into his own 'intuitive research into the *unique form of continuity in space'*. To see how Boccioni did try to attempt this synthesis of Cubism and Futurism, while trying to deliberately colonize an area under-exploited by the Cubists, we must turn to his sculptures and his *Technical Manifesto of Futurist Sculpture* (Chipp. pp.298–304). Read this Manifesto now.

You may be surprised, in view of the apparent rejection of any interest in the art of the past in the first Manifesto, that Boccioni devotes part of this text to a thumbnail sketch of sculpture through the ages and the work of recent sculptors (Meunier, Bourdelle, Rodin and the Italian Medardo Rosso). Part of the reason may be Boccioni's nationalistic defence of the latter but it is also the case that Boccioni was becoming increasingly concerned in his writings to 'place' his own work in the history of modern art as he saw it. Much of this document will be familiar to you, from the earlier manifestoes. You have already seen how Hamilton selected the fourth Conclusion (use of diverse and unusual materials) as a significant Futurist innovation. It is surprising, therefore, that Boccioni made little use of this idea in his own work, apart from his *Fusion of a Head and Window,* 1911–12, discussed by Hamilton (p.287) (**Pl. VI. 11**).

Boccioni's main concern was simply to extend Futurist principles into sculpture, as Medardo Rosso, so he argued, had extended the principles of Impressionism into sculpture. But how could a 'sculpture of environment' be tackled? Once again, Boccioni found himself faced with a technical problem as a direct result of formulating a tactical objective. Parisian critics were mystified by the Sculpture Manifesto:

> And the end of it will be that the new sculptures will be made to speak: 'Daddy,
> Mummy' and 'Long live Marinetti'.
> (F. Divoire, in *L'Intransigéant,* 1 October 1912.)

And, just as the critics had misinterpreted, wilfully or otherwise, the Futurists' ideas about motion in Futurist dynamism, they had a field day with the 'style of movement' in sculpture:

> This summer there will be an exposition which will cause a fuss. It is a show of
> Futurist statuettes conceived according to the theories expressed in a recent man-
> ifesto. The statuettes will be articulated and mobile and they will be activated by a
> motor which will be specially installed.
> (A. Warnod, in *Comoedia,* 22 February 1913.)

Boccioni's exhibition of sculpture took place in June 1913 at the Gallerie La Boetie, and Apollinaire, for one, welcomed it with reservations:

> His researches into form still seem to be interpreted, not to say modelled, after
> nature so that the effort to give primacy, rightly, to the architectural, is almost
> entirely lost.
> (G. Apollinaire, in *L'Intransigéant,* 21 June 1913.)

Apollinaire went on to praise Boccioni's 'many novelties', including the variety of materials and 'sculptural simultaneity', but in focusing on the 'architectural', for which there is an excuse in the Sculpture Manifesto (Chipp, p.301, line 31), he is stressing the element of Cubist analysis in Boccioni's work at the expense of the 'style of movement'. Indeed, he picked out some of the drawings as particularly worthy of attention. Now, if you compare the drawing for the sculpture, *Development of a Bottle in Space* (Pl.VI.12), with the actual sculpture (Pl.VI.13), you will notice precisely this difference between a Cubist style and what Boccioni seems to have been driving at in the Sculpture Manifesto. The drawing even includes circles with measurements, as if what is shown is an architectural plan. The sculpture eliminates almost all the background detail (the houses, plane of the table top, etc.) and concentrates on the spiralling forms of the bottle. He seems to be trying to develop the 'central nucleus of the object' according to the 'new laws, that is, the new forms that link it invisibly but mathematically to the *apparent plastic infinite* and to the *internal plastic infinite*' (cf. Chipp, p.300, top). The 'problem' Boccioni has set himself, based once again on Bergson's ideas of intuition, is purely ontological, to do with 'what reality is'. The problem is that if you believe that reality can be grasped only in memory and by intuition and that matter and perception are the enemy of this higher comprehension, it is very difficult to use a 'solid' material like clay or bronze to convey your intentions. Sculpture, being more tangibly material and less obviously conventionalized than painting, makes this difficulty all the more apparent.

From 1912–13, Boccioni put a great deal of effort into creating a definitive Futurist sculpture which, while using the technical ideas in the Sculpture Manifesto, would also stand for 'Futurist Man' — an image of man compatible with Futurist rhetoric about violent energy and revolutionary impact. A series of large striding figures in plaster, most of them destroyed, have been recorded in photographs, and they trace the evolution of *The Unique Forms of Continuity in Space.*

▶ Look at these four sculptures (Pls.VI.14–17) (*Synthesis of Human Dynamism, Muscles at Speed, Spiral Expansion of Muscles in Movement,* and *Unique Forms of Continuity in Space*). How does Boccioni adopt the formal devices of Cubist painting to sculpture compatible with his Technical Manifesto? ◀

▷ *Synthesis of Human Dynamism* retains some of the pictorial devices of *Fusion of Head and Window:* a window frame is superimposed on the head. There is a Cubist combination of fragments of realistic detail (hair, ear, belly button, etc.) with an apparatus of planes and surfaces. The legs seem to display an example of '*movimentismo*' of a cinematographic kind: the calf appears to be repeated in several lines as if caught at several points on its trajectory. The *Muscles at Speed* reads more like a sculptural equivalent of a Futurist painting: the 'atmosphere' between the legs is treated in as solid a way as the bodily members. The concentration is now on the main forms of the muscles, abstracted into flowing forms. As a free-standing sculpture, Boccioni's work could be seen as having the same two-dimensionality that Boccioni identified as a failing in the sculpture of Medardo Rosso. This two-dimensionality is considerably reduced in the *Spiral Expansion of Muscles in Movement,* which seems to adapt the formal discoveries of the *Development of a Bottle in Space.* The basic form of a striding man is now clearly revealed in mass, and this carcase is then expanded and developed to give the muscular effort its most exaggerated impact. The finished version adds some flowing forms to the calves suggesting a blur of movement, or an atmospheric 'bow-wave' representing movement through space. ◁

We will return, in Part 3, to the question of Boccioni's reasons for putting so much effort into subjects — the still life, the standing figure — which he continually denigrated in the work of the Cubists. We can only look at one example of Boccioni's mature paintings of 1912–13, *Elasticità* (Pl.VI.18), which, once again, represents a conventional painters' subject — the equestrian figure. Carrà also chose this subject at this time (Pl.VI.19) and the comparison is instructive about the different approaches of the two artists. It's worth noting that a furious cavalry charge was an image used by Bergson to describe the furious rush of life conquering matter. Carrà's drawing stresses the jagged juxtaposition of fragments of detail, suggesting mechanical analogies (pivots, axles), while Boccioni tries in his painting to suggest movement and power through similar methods to the sculptures — flowing curves and fleshy forms that we read as muscles. He seems to want us to empathize with the force of the animal and rider through bodily sensation, just as Bergson suggested that it is the bodily sensations of the arm that convey the sense of movement from point A to point B.

It should be clear by now that Boccioni's interests only partly coincided with those of Marinetti. The stress on intuition and emotion in his writings and the determination to solve specific 'problems' set by the history of modern art as he understood it, led him to drop almost all the allusions to urban change and industrialization. In 1915, Boccioni left for the front in the general patriotic fervour stimulated by Marinetti and the Interventionist demonstrations. But his experiences sobered him up and in a letter of August 1916 he wrote:

> From this existence, I will emerge with contempt for everything which is not art. Everything I see now is a game compared to a good drawing, a beautiful poem or a correct harmony. Compared with these, it's merely a question of mechanics, habit, patience, memory. There is only art.
>
> (Extract from a letter published by H. Walden, *Der Sturm*, September 1916.)

And, in his painting, Boccioni had already abandoned the Futurist dynamism of *Elasticità* for a series of portraits and interiors heavily derived from Cézanne (Pl.VI.20). By this time, too, Carrà and Severini were also preparing to abandon Futurism. A new generation of Futurist painters (the 'second Futurism') took up Marinetti's ideas, in a more prosaic and overtly political form after the First World War. The tension between Marinetti's aims, and those of the painters, is the main subject of Part 3.

3 Futurism, Fascism and Modernism

To understand the critical response to Futurism up until the Second World War we will have to look more closely at Marinetti's political and ideological views, as these attracted more attention than the work produced by the painters. We will also have to examine the place of Boccioni and the painters within this ideology and the problems they posed for them. The subsequent historiography, and the issues it raises, should then become clearer.

Marinetti eventually joined the Fascist party and became a member of the Fascist Academy, finishing his days in the pathetic and horrific Republic of Salo which survived for 100 days during the collapse of Fascism in Italy in 1944. This makes the task of identifying his political and ideological position particularly difficult. His militarism ('war, sole hygiene of the world', the 'beautiful ideas which kill') was also shared by many anarchists in Italy. And Marinetti had close links with anarchists like Ottavio Dinale who, confusingly, were also ardently nationalistic, preaching intervention in the First World War in 1915. Many Italian Socialists were aggressive nationalists who, under the guise of 'anti-boche' feeling, campaigned for the return of the 'Irredentist' territories (Trent, Trieste and the Tyrol) still in the hands of Austria. This was partly because extremists of right and left united in attacking government policy that sought to maintain and renew the Triple Alliance between Italy, Germany and Austria-Hungary (1882) which alone seemed to guarantee economic prosperity. In the event, Italy had it both ways, conquering Libya and Tripolitania from the Turks in 1911–12 with Austrian compliance while deserting her allies in 1915 to join Britain and France in the War. So, when Marinetti staged demonstrations and public confrontations against the Austrians, he was tapping a very wide vein of nationalist feelings, while effectively helping to subvert government policy. Marinetti's militaristic nationalism was probably closer to his real interests than any of his cultural activities. When the war with Libya was declared, he called on his Futurist colleagues:

> While the war lasts, let us set aside our verses, brushes, chisels and orchestras. Genius is embarking on a red holiday. Today we can admire nothing except the formidable symphony of shrapnel and the crazy sculptures which our inspired artillery throws up in the enemy ranks.
>
> (F. Marinetti, *Political Manifesto of Futurism*, October 1911.)

And he seems to have been disappointed that the Futurist painters did not in fact join him at the siege of Adrianopolis, preferring instead to prepare the Exhibition of Futurist Painting of February 1912. Marinetti was a natural hooligan, he actually enjoyed the fights and bruises of the Futurist evenings, and was decorated twice for reckless bravery in the First World War. Furthermore, his allusions to 'the destructive gesture of the anarchist' fell on ears already sensitized by the writings of the Syndicalist, Georges Sorel, and the sympathies of the French Symbolists and Italian Divisionists. In the confusion, it was difficult for contemporaries to sort out fashionable postures from real politics. Camille Le Mercier d'Erm, once again, saw through Marinetti better than most:

3 Futurism, Fascism and Modernism

As for the 'destructive gesture of the anarchists', have a care Marinetti! . . . If I'm not mistaken, you belong to that cursed class, generally known as capitalist, on whose heads, barring fear of the gendarme who is the beginning of wisdom, the bombs will rain down like hail or wedding confetti.

(*Les Argonautes,* **II,** 10, 1909.)

As the links between Marinetti and post-First World War Fascism have influenced critical reactions in Italy to Futurism, we must attempt to see what these links consisted of. Up until 1913, most of the harshest critics of Futurism came from the political Right, responding to the general tone of Marinetti's writings rather than their content. But as Benedetto Croce wrote, at a time when he was still approving of Mussolini's Fascism:

Whoever has a sense of historical connections will realize that the ideal origin of Fascism can be found in Futurism. In that determination to go down into the piazza, to impose its own views, to close the mouths of dissidents, to be unafraid of crowds and brawls, in that thirst for the new, that eagerness to break with all traditions, in that exultation of youth; this was Futurism and it spoke to the heart of the veterans of the trenches. . . . I used to deny that from Futurism, with its collective, opinionated, harsh and guttersnipe ways, any poetry could come. . . but I did not deny and indeed recognize the practical and pragmatic character of Futurism.

(Benedetto Croce, *La Stampa,* 15 May, 1924.)

As we will see, very similar arguments were used to defend Futurism as a revolutionary movement by Antonio Gramsci. Marinetti's third Political Manifesto, of 1918, showed how unrealistic his grasp of politics really was. At a time when his *'fasci di combattimento'* (gangs of veteran soldiers anxious to assert a new order in post-war Italy) were roaming the streets, beating up their opponents and destabilizing the government, Marinetti was advocating abolishing the Church, marriage, parliament, the whole land tenure system and proposing a whole-scale re-ordering of society around the twin principles of personal courage and passionate nationalism. In March, 1919, the *fasci di combattimento* were absorbed into the Fascist party. However, when the Fascists suffered a severe electoral defeat in 1920, Mussolini quickly dropped the hotch-potch of confused and idealistic supporters to make the deals with landed wealth, big business, the Church and, eventually, the King, that brought him to power two years later. Marinetti's initial response was horrified renunciation, particularly at Mussolini's populist appeals to the authority of a 'third' Imperial Rome, and the prestige of the classical heritage in Italy. By the time Marinetti returned to the Fascist fold, the straight-jacket of Mussolini's corporate state had made a nonsense of all his previously held convictions.

It is important to recognize the essentially aesthetic quality of Marinetti's politics while also being aware of the very real political constituency of some of the elements that composed it. A startling index of the ambiguity of Marinetti's political activities can be gauged from five articles written by Antonio Gramsci, the founder and theoretician of Italian Communism. Although Marinetti had written a very explicit attack on the Left in 1920, 'Beyond Communism', Gramsci was able to write in his paper, *Ordine Nuovo* (5 January 1921):

The Futurists destroyed, destroyed, destroyed, without worrying whether their new creations were all in all superior to those they demolished. . . they had a clear and precise conception that our era, the era of big industry, of the great workers' cities, of intense and tumultuous life, had to have new forms of art, philosophy, customs, language; this was their clearly revolutionary concept, and an absolutely Marxist one. . . The Futurists in their field, the field of culture, are revolutionaries; in this field, in terms of creativity, it is unlikely that the working class will be able to do more than the Futurists for a long time.

And he told Trotsky, in 1922:

> Before the War, the Futurists enjoyed a certain popularity with the workers. . .
> During the manifestations of Futurist art in the theatres of the large Italian cities,
> it used to be that the workers defended the Futurists from the assaults of the
> half-aristocrats and half-bourgeois bands of youths.

A recent critic, however, made a balanced judgment when he defined Marinetti's interest as essentially sensationalist, concerned with action for its own sake:

> Italian Futurism erects no plan for the future, it gives no model for a future
> society. Its activity is entirely immersed in the struggle against the ghosts of the
> past. They wanted change, the leap in the dark, but the reality of individual
> actions was dictated only by the obscure desire to accelerate the march of history.
> (Lista, p. 16.)

Marinetti's attitudes are those of the decadent, the man of leisure from a secure background who craves excitement. In this, as in many other details, the imagery of the first Manifesto is precise. Art, politics and life could all be likened to a dangerous and murderous drive through the night.

But while Marinetti's personality makes all this comprehensible, it left the other Futurists in a difficult position. They had no security, no reputation, no venue to publicize and sell their wares. Futurism provided the publicity to make good these deficiencies; as Hamilton points out, many Futurist paintings had been sold by the time the exhibition of 1912 had finished its spell at the *Der Sturm* gallery in the summer. However, from a political point of view, Boccioni, Carrà and Russolo were unlikely converts to Marinetti's band. Russolo was a pacifist with anarchist sympathies who, after accepting Marinetti's warmongering of 1914–15, reacted and eventually left Italy in 1926 to escape Fascism. Carrà, in 1909, was an active Syndicalist, with many anarchist friends, who seems to have given in completely to Marinetti's ideas, writing, on the eve of the War:

> Today the bourgeois favourable to war is certainly more revolutionary than the
> so-called revolutionary with his neutralism. The former takes risks and acts while
> the latter, the so-called anarchist, is harmful to life and progress because, in real-
> ity, he sacrifices nothing to them.
> (C. Carrà, *Guerrapittura*, 1915.)

And Boccioni was reported as saying, in 1909:

> That he admired the leader of the Futurists, and that in art he sympathized with
> the programme he had devised, although he reserved politics for his own Marxist
> convictions.
> (L. Altamare, quoted in *Studio International*, April 1973.)

And yet Boccioni followed Marinetti into the demonstrations for the Irredentist territories and, in 1915, the Interventionist riots. Whatever reservations any of the Futurists might have had about Marinetti's views, they did not reveal them publicly.

Critics of Futurism have been faced, therefore, with the problem of trying to evaluate what the Modernist tradition presents as formally progressive (in terms of 'technical innovations') in the face of a political ideology discredited by Fascism. During the 1920s and 1930s, Futurism was largely ignored, partly because of these political associations. In America, where several Futurist paintings had been bought by collectors generally indifferent to European political trends, it was easier to recuperate the purely formal innovations of the work. Joshua C. Taylor, for example, wrote:

> The nature of the Futurist impulse in politics. . . should not influence the assess-
> ment of its achievement in art.

This was in the influential book accompaying the Futurist exhibition at the Museum of Modern Art, New York, in 1961. Earlier, in 1949, a major exhibition had been held in the Museum of Modern Art, 'Twentieth Century Italian Painting and Sculpture', which included the work of Balla, Boccioni and Severini. As a result of this exhibition, *The City Rises* and *Unique Forms of Continuity in Space* were purchased by the Museum. In 1950, the Tate had an exhibition of Italian art in which Futurist work was shown and described as 'bang up to date'. In the same year, the Venice Biennale showed Futurist and Cubist works, and there was a major retrospective of Futurism at Bologna in the following year. In 1954, Sidney Janis's book, *Abstract and Surrealist Art in America,* included the following passage:

> That the twentieth century pioneer American painters — Stella, Demuth, Feiniger, Sheeler and MacDonald-Wright — should have been drawn to many of the principles of Futurism is not surprising. The machine and its multiplex activity, speed, force, dynamics, are salt to the American spirit, and many of our serious painters generously flavoured the character of their work with the valid pictorial ideas from Futurist sources.
>
> (Cited in R. T. Clough, *Futurism: The Study of a Modern Art Movement,* pp.238–9.)

We have seen how specific to the Italian context Marinetti's interest in machines and industrialization was, and how Futurist ideology was opposed to American positivism in all its aspects. And yet the art historians of the 1950s and 1960s were able to justify Futurism for its healthy regard for 'the machine'.

In Italy, the defence of Futurist ideology took a little longer, but the collapse of Fascism had released a flood of memorabilia and paintings from the families of the original Futurist painters which could not be ignored in the art market, particularly in the face of American and British interest. In 1958, a major publication, the two-volume *Archivi del Futurismo,* reprinted a large number of manifestoes and articles from the period that made a study of the ideological roots of Futurism more accessible. From that date onwards, Italian critics at least have had to construct arguments to account for the proto-Fascist elements in Marinetti's writings, many of them, like the literary critic Enrico Falqui, explaining its excesses as a reaction to the provincialism and isolation of Italian culture before the First World War.

Those writers who, like John Golding, have attempted to put together the work of the Futurist painters with the Marinettian ideology that held the movement together, have experienced great difficulties in presenting Futurism as simply 'progressive'. Describing Boccioni's *Unique Forms of Continuity in Space,* Golding wrote:

> . . . and there is something both awe-inspiring and a little frightening about the vision of this Futurist demi-God striding sightlessly through space above the heads of a public that Boccioni, in his letters, talks of with hatred and contempt — 'scum', he says at one point 'whom we must lead into slavery': The influence of visual Futurism was almost wholly positive and liberating, but to emphasize only the forward-looking elements of the movement as all art historians have done, is to falsify the total picture . . . But for the first time in twentieth century art, the sources of official Fascist imagery are hinted at, and the *Unique Forms of Continuity in Space* is a revolutionary work which carries within it the seeds of reaction.
>
> (J. Golding, *Boccioni's Unique Forms of Continuity in Space,* 1972.)

Clearly, a proto-Fascist ideology supporting a 'revolutionary' and positive artistic achievement poses problems for those who see a necessary connection between the 'advance' of modern art and socialism (or any other political or ideological position). Golding obviously sees a contradiction between the 'liberating' effects of 'visual Futurism' — its place presumably in the development of modern art as codified by Modernism — and the anti-democratic views of the Futurists. But this begs the question of whether innovation in art has any necessary connection with political revolution. To describe the *Unique Forms* as 'revolutionary' raises similar issues to those in Gramsci's editorial of January 1921, quoted above. But, for Gramsci, the Futurists were praiseworthy for the actual, material destabilization of bourgeois

31

society by cultural means. For Golding, 'revolutionary' appears to mean little more than 'forward-looking' or 'formally innovative' and yet the term is used in contradistinction to the 'seeds of reaction'. The whole relationship of art and politics will be discussed further in Blocks VIII and IX and you should think through these issues for yourself. As historians, however, our task is to identify, within the limits of the available evidence, what measurable effects works of art and ideas can be shown to have had on the whole range of thought and action, including politics and art. And it is mainly due to the presence of key Futurist works, including this one, in American collections that has tended to separate their 'visual' history from the history of Italian politics.

The tradition of Modernism which subtracts paintings from the ideological and material conditions that prompted them is as inadequate as a tradition that seeks to show paintings as mere reflections of ideology. The case of Futurism makes this particularly evident, as it is hard to sort out any one set of ideas that everyone agreed on and responded to. The Futurist painters accepted Marinetti partly from personal persuasion and partly from expediency. And it is clear, from Boccioni's writings, as well as his work, that he considered other, and contradictory arguments to those of Marinetti as necessary for defending Futurist art. We have seen, in the Sculpture Manifesto, how he offered an historical framework for his work. In an article he laid out a schematic history of western art in four great stages, each with its 'elaboration, apex, transformation and ultimate state'. In doing so he reflected the idealist tradition of art historians like Wolfflin and Burckhardt. These stages were:

1 Greek plastic abstraction (physical exterior centre of the Universe).

2 Christian plastic abstraction (passage from exterior to the interior).

3 Naturalistic plastic abstraction (exteriorization of the interior environment, landscape).

4 Futurist plastic abstraction (interior and exterior appear in simultaneous interpretation).

(Boccioni, 'For Italian ignorance', 15 August, 1913.)

Under the third phase, he divided up the Impressionists and the Cubists into two streams: those like Cézanne, Picasso and the Gleizes–Metzinger group, who concentrated on form and the products of intellect, and those who, like Monet, Seurat and Matisse, were more concerned with sensation and colour. Futurism is presented as the synthesis of these two strands, combining the opposed faculties of intellect and intuition (Bergson again). The 'apex' of this last phase was described as 'Dynamism — Subject — States of Mind', but Boccioni clearly found it impossible to imagine how this idealist scheme could be continued.

Marinetti imposed severe strains on his colleagues. He would perhaps have liked the painters to limit themselves to illustrating the themes of Futurist ideology as he defined them. But for an ambitious artist like Boccioni who wanted to assert his standing in terms of 'rivals' in France, it wasn't as simple as that. His whole understanding of art was formed by the idealist notion of a progression of ideas towards an ultimate synthesis.

Saddled with the then fashionable aesthetics of Bergson and forced to assimilate the complex and difficult style of Cubism, in order to 'defeat' it, he found himself drawn into an increasingly sterile debate over primacy and invention. In articles like 'The Futurists plagiarized in France' (1 April 1913) he attempted to show that Orphism 'is nothing other than an elegant masquerade of the fundamental principles of Futurism'. Meanwhile, his own work was increasingly devoted to the kind of subject matter, as we have seen, that he had attacked in the Cubists' work. To understand Boccioni, we have to see him caught between an 'autonomous' competitiveness with the French Cubists, his own response to Italian conditions and the imposed ideological imperatives of Marinetti.

Conclusion

Much of the interest of Futurism lies in its importance to Italian cultural history. The public impact of Futurist ideology played a significant role in Italian nationalist politics and the birth of Fascism. In the Modernist account of the history of modern art, Futurism fits in awkwardly. The stress on 'modern' subject matter, intuition, symbolism, dynamism and 'states of mind' in the manifestoes hardly fits the Modernist formula, and yet the paintings and sculptures clearly respond to the techniques of some, at least, of the Cubists and Orphists. The confusion in French–Italian relationships caused by jealousies and rivalries is highlighted by the case of Apollinaire. After criticizing the Futurists consistently, Apollinaire ended up writing a Futurist Manifesto, *L'Antitradition Futuriste,* 29 June 1913, which many French critics considered a joke. In January 1913, Apollinaire had dismissed Futurism as an off-shoot of Orphism (lecture in Berlin), taking sides with his friend Delaunay in his wrangle with Boccioni.

Futurism certainly left its mark on the Parisian avant-garde, contributing to the diversification of Cubism after 1912. In television programme 14, we will look more closely at the impact of Futurist ideas and imagery throughout Europe.

References and further reading

(All translations in text by Tim Benton).

Apollinaire, Guillaume, article in *L'Intransigéant*, 21 June 1913

Ballo, G., *Boccioni: La Vita e l'Opera*, Il Saggiatore, Milan, 1964.

Barocchi, P., *Testimonianze e Polemiche Figurative in Italia, del Divisionismo*, Florence 1974.

Birolli, Zeno (ed.), *Boccioni: Scritti editi e inediti*, Feltrinelli, Milan 1971.

Boccioni, Umberto, 'For Italian ignorance' 15 August 1913.

Clough, Rosa, *Futurism: The Study of a Modern Art Movement*, Greenwood, New York 1961.

Croce, Benedetto, article in *La Stampa*, 15 May 1924.

Dell'Arco, Mauricio, *Balla Pre-Futurista*, Bulzoni, Rome, 1970.

de Micheli, Mario, 'The political ideology of Futurism' in *Studio International*, April 1973.

Divoire, F., 'Sculpture must be open or closed' in *L'Intransigéant*, 1 October 1912.

Golding, John, 'Boccioni's *Unique Forms of Continuity in Space*', University of Newcastle, Charlton Lecture No. 54, 1972.

Gramsci, Antonio, editorial in *Ordine Nuovo*, 5 January 1921.

Grubicy, V., 'La *Maternità* di Gaetano Previati' in *Cronaca d'Arte*, No. 22, 12 May 1891.

Janis, Sidney, *Abstract and Surrealist Art in America*, 1954.

Jannini, P.A., *La Fortuna del Futurismo in Francia*, Bulzoni, Rome 1979.

Le Mercier d'Erm, Camille, in *Les Argonautes*, II, 10, 1909.

Lista, G., *Marinetti et le Futurisme*, Le Age d'Homme, Lausanne 1977.

Marinetti, Filippo, 'Let's murder the moonbeams', in *Poesia*, Nos. 7,8 and 9, 1909.

Marinetti, Filippo, *Political Manifesto of Futurism*, October 1911.

Mitchell, B. R., *European Historical Statistics*, 2nd rev.edn., Macmillan, 1981.

Mussolini, Benito, *Il Popolo di Trento*, 9 July 1909.

Previati, Gaetano, *Principii Scientifici del Divisionismo*, Bocca, Turin, 1905–6.

Russell, Bertrand, *History of Western Philosophy*, Unwin, 1979.

Soffici, Ardengo, 'Cézanne' in *La Voce*, June 1908.

Soffici, Ardengo, 'Impressionism and Italian painting' in *La Voce*, March 1909.

Walden, Herwarth, 'Letter from Boccioni', in *Der Sturm*, September 1916.

Warnod, André in *Comoedia*, 22 February 1913.

Appendix A

Select list of Futurist exhibitions

Free Art Exhibition, Chamber of Labour, Milan, April 1911.

Futurist Painting, Bernheim–Jeune Gallery, Paris, February 1912.

Futurist Painting, Sackville Gallery, London, March 1912.

Futurist Painting, Der Sturm Gallery, Berlin, April–May 1912.

Futurist Painting, Georges Giroux Gallery, Brussels, June 1912.

Futurist Painting, Rotterdamsche Kunstring, Rotterdam, May–June 1913.

Futurist Painting, 'Erster deutsche Herbstsalon, Der Sturm, Berlin, 1913.

Boccioni Sculptures, Galerie la Boetie, Paris, June–July 1913.

First Exhibition of Futurist Paintings, Teatro Costanzi, Rome, February–March 1913.

Futurist Painting, (organized by *Lacerba*), Florence, November 1913–January 1914.

Futurist Sculpture: Boccioni, Sprovieri Gallery, Rome, December 1913.

Grand National Futurist Exhibition, Galleria Centrale d'Arte, Milan, March 1919.

Large Futurist entry in San Francisco Panama–Pacific International Exposition, 1915.

Substantial Futurist exhibits at the *Venice Biennale,* 1926/28/30/32.

Italian Futurist Painters, Galerie 23, Paris, December 1929.

Twentieth Century Italian Painting, MOMA, New York, 1949.

The Signatories of the First Futurist Manifesto, Sala VI, Venice Biennale, 1950.

Italian Art, Tate Gallery, organized by Milanese Society of the Amici de Brera, 1950.

Futurist and Metaphysical Painting, Kunsthaus, Zurich, 1950.

National Exhibition of Futurist Painting, Bologna, 1954.

Futurism, São Paolo, Brazil, 1953.

Futurism, Balla, Boccioni, Carrà, Russolo, Severini, Sidney Janis Gallery, New York, 1954.

Futurism, Palazzo Barberini, Rome, June 1959.

The Futurists, Städlischen Galerie, Munich, 1959–60.

Historical Exhibition of Futurism, Rooms I and IV, XXX Venice Biennale, 1960.

Futurist Paintings and Drawings, Famiglia Artistica, Milan, February 1960.

Futurism, Museum of Modern Art, New York, May–September 1961.

Futurism 1909–1919, University of Newcastle-upon-Tyne, 1972 and Royal Scottish Academy, Edinburgh, 1972.

Appendix B

List of principal Futurist Manifestoes 1909–1919

Unless otherwise stated, these manifestoes were first published as leaflets by Marinetti in Milan. The titles are translated to indicate their content.

F. T. MARINETTI, 'The Foundation and Manifesto of Futurism', *Le Figaro,* 20 February 1909.

F. T. MARINETTI, 'Let's murder the moonbeams', 10 April 1909, *Poesia,* reprinted in Marinetti's anthology, *Le Futurisme,* Sansot, 1911.

F. T. MARINETTI, 'First Political Manifesto', 1909.

F. T. MARINETTI, 'Futurist Proclamation to the Spanish', *Prometeo,* 1910, Madrid.

U. BOCCIONI, C. CARRÀ, L. RUSSOLO, G. BALLA and G. SEVERINI (the last two signatures replaced those of Aroldo Bonzagni and Romolo Romani after the first edition), 'Manifesto of the Futurist Painters', 11 February 1910.

U. BOCCIONI, C. CARRÀ, L. RUSSOLO, G. BALLA and G. SEVERINI, 'Futurist Painting: Technical Manifesto', 11 April 1910.

F. T. MARINETTI, U. BOCCIONI, C. CARRÀ and L. RUSSOLO, 'Against *Passé* Venice', 27 April 1910.

F. B. PRATELLA, 'Manifesto of the Futurist Musicians', 11 January 1911.

F. B. PRATELLA, 'Futurist Music. Technical Manifesto', 29 March 1911.

F. T. MARINETTI, 'Second Political Manifesto', 11 October 1911.

C. MAUCLAIR, 'The Futurists and Young Italy', *La Dépêche de Toulouse,* 30 October 1911.

VALENTINE DE SAINT-PONT, 'Manifesto of Futurist Woman', 25 March 1912.

U. BOCCIONI, 'Futurist Sculpture', 11 April 1912.

F. T. MARINETTI, 'Technical Manifesto of Futurist Literature,' 11 May 1912.

RAYNYST, 'Futurist Painting in Belgium', June 1912.

C. RUSSOLO, 'The Art of Noises', 11 March 1913.

F. T. MARINETTI, 'Wireless — Imagination and Words in Liberty', 11 May 1913.

G. APOLLINAIRE, 'The Futurist Anti-Tradition', 29 June 1913.

C. CARRÀ, 'Painting, Sounds, Noises and Smells', 11 August 1913.

F. T. MARINETTI, 'Music Hall, Futurist Manifesto', 29 September 1913, in the *Daily Mail,* 21 November 1913.

A. PALAZZESCHI, 'Counter-Pain, Futurist Manifesto', 29 December 1913.

F. T. MARINETTI, 'Geometric and Mechanical Splendour in Words in Liberty', 15 March 1914.

A. SANT'ELIA, 'Futurist Architecture, Manifesto', 11 July 1914.

F. T. MARINETTI (with C. R. W. NEVINSON), 'Vital English Art, Futurist Manifesto', *Lacerba,* 15 July 1914.

G. BALLA, 'Anti-Neutralist Clothing, Futurist Manifesto', 11 September 1914.

F. T. MARINETTI, U. BOCCIONI, L. RUSSOLO, M. SIRONI and A. SANT'ELIA, 'Italian Pride, Futurist Manifesto', January 1915.

G. BALLA and F. DEPERO, 'Futurist Reconstruction of the Universe', 2 March 1915.

U. BOCCIONI, 'Manifesto to the Southern Painters,' 5 February 1916.

F. T. MARINETTI, 'The New Moral Religion of Speed', May 1916.

Appendix C

Some notices in the French press of Futurist events, exhibitions or publications (extracted from Jannini *op. cit.*).

C. Etienne, '"Futurism". The idea of Mr. F. T. Marinetti. A new literary school — a challenge to the stars', *La Liberté*, Paris, 24 February 1909.

M. D., 'Futurism', *Journal des Débats,* Paris, 25 February 1909.

G. De Pawlowski, 'The land of the dead', *Comoedia,* Paris, 26 February 1909.

G. Timmory, 'A cheerful life', *L'Echo de Paris,* Paris, 26 February 1909.

(The four notices above were just some of those, hostile as well as approving, which were republished by Marinetti in *Poesia.)*

Touny-Lerys, M. Dhano, G. Gaudion, 'Primitivism', *Poésie,* Toulouse, winter 1909; the editors of this journal responded to Futurism with their own movement.

'Futurism', *Les Guêpes,* March 1909, reprints Marinetti's circular letter accompanying the Futurist Manifesto, alongside the reply of Jules Romains.

'The Marinetti–Hirsch duel', *Paris-Journal,* 17 April 1909 (an account of a duel in the Parc des Princes in which Hirsch was wounded).

'From Futurism to Primitivism', *Poésie,* Toulouse (publishes reactions from provençal writers to the conflict between the two movements).

Le Wattman (no title), *L'Intransigéant,* Paris, 17 May 1910 (commentary on the Painters' Manifesto).

Anon., 'Manifesto of the Futurist painters', *Comoedia,* Paris, 18 May 1910.

G. Apollinaire, 'The Futurist painters', *Mercure de France,* Paris, 16 November 1911. (Without having seen any Futurist paintings, recounts the fight between the Milanese Futurists and Soffici in a Florentine café.)

A. Alexandre, 'The minor exhibitions', *Le Figaro,* 4 February 1912 (note on the Bernheim–Jeune Gallery Futurist show, describing the paintings as 'influenced by Cubism. . . which the Futurists deny').

Short notes on the exhibition were also published in *Excelsior, Gil Blas, Paris-Journal, Comoedia, L'Intransigéant,* and *Le Petit Bleu.* They note the crowds at the opening, the turbulent response to the paintings and the influence of Cubism and Unanimism, e.g. Apollinaire (*L'Intransigéant,* 7 February 1912):

> The Futurists are young painters whom we might respect were it not for the violence of their declarations and the insolence of their manifestoes which set aside the indulgence which we might otherwise feel for them. They declare themselves 'absolutely opposed' to the art of the extreme French schools but are nothing but their imitators. Look at Boccioni, who seems to me to be the most gifted of the Futurist painters. Picasso's influence is as undeniable on him as it is on all contemporary painting . . . The titles of the Futurist paintings seem frequently to be lifted from the vocabulary of Unanimism . . . The young Futurist painters can rival some of our avant-garde artists but they are still nothing but feeble imitators of a Picasso or a Derain and, as for grace, they haven't a clue.

And, in *Le Petit Bleu* (9 February 1912), he wrote:

> It's in what separates them (the Futurists) from the new French painters that can be found what seems to me to be the damnation of Futurist art . . . The Futurists have virtually no plastic preoccupations . . . They want to paint 'States of Mind'. It's the most dangerous painting you could think of. It will lead the Futurist painters to become nothing but illustrators. Nevertheless, the Futurist painters' exhibition will teach our young painters to have more guts than they have had to date. Without guts, the Futurists would never have dared to exhibit their endeavours in such an imperfect state. It will also show them how far they are still in the lead over their rivals in Italy and all other nations . . . As for Futurist painting, it raises a few smiles in Paris, but it shouldn't make the Italians smile, or it would be too bad for them.

G. Kahn, 'Art', *Mercure de France,* 16 February 1912 (very positive review of the exhibition).

E. J. B., 'Futurist Sculpture', *Le Temps,* 30 September 1912 (about the Sculpture Manifesto):

> These people are quite simply delightful. They could write, paint, sculpt, like everyone else (. . .) They go to the trouble . . . to find the most abracadabra-ish formula . . . When it comes to sculpture or painting, Boccioni is tremendous, that's to say, Futurist . . . And in truth, if we understood it (the Manifesto) it would be much less amusing.

G. Apollinaire, 'Futurism', *L'Intermédiaire des Chercheurs et Curieux,* Paris, 10 October 1912:

> The Cubists paint objects . . . as they represent themselves, and their work is extremely lucid and pure. The Futurists, who disperse the different aspects of an object in their canvases with the numerous feelings which provoke these aspects easily arrive at confusion . . . Arbitrariness is the order of the day in Futurist art despite the explanations and manifestoes.

G. Apollinaire, 'First Exhibition of Futurist Sculpture by the Futurist painter and sculptor Boccioni', *L'Intransigéant,* Paris, 21 June 1913 (see text of this block for extract from this favourable review)

Notices of the show appeared in *Le Figaro, L'Eclair, L'Homme libre, Comoedia, Le Radical, Gazette de France, Paris-Midi, La Vie Parisienne, Paris-Journal, La Republique Française,* and *Mercure de France.* Most of these notices welcomed the absence of violent demonstrations at the exhibition and accompanying lectures by Boccioni and Marinetti and generally mark a warmer response than that for the Bernheim-Jeune exhibition. It is clear that Boccioni was becoming accepted in Paris.